FACT CAT

ANGLO-SAXONS

Izzi Howell

6000037872 9

Northamptonshire Libraries & Information Services NC

Askews & Holts

All rights reserved
ISBN: 978 0 7502 9939 8
Dewey Number: 942'.01-dc23

10 9 8 7 6 5 4 3 2 1

FSC
MIX
Paper from responsible sources
FSC® C104740
www.fsc.org

Wayland
An imprint of Hachette Children's Group
Part of Hodder & Stoughton
Carmelite House
50 Victoria Embankment
London EC4Y 0DZ

An Hachette UK Company
www.hachette.co.uk
www.hachettechildrens.co.uk

A catalogue for this title is available from
the British Library
Printed and bound in China

Produced for Wayland by
White-Thomson Publishing Ltd
www.wtpub.co.uk

Editor: Izzi Howell
Design: Rocket Design (East Anglia) Ltd
Fact Cat illustrations: Shutterstock/Julien Troneur
Other illustrations: Stefan Chabluk
Consultant: Kate Ruttle

Picture and illustration credits:
Corbis: Jean Williamson/LOOP IMAGES/Loop Images 9,
Michael Nicholson 14, Lebrecht/Lebrecht Music & Arts
16; iStock: lightphoto cover, stevegeer 6, lightphoto 17,
duncan1890 21; Stefan Chabluk: 5; Shutterstock: De Visu 4,
ArtMari 11, Daniele Pietrobelli 13, Marbury 15, Philip Bird LRPS
CPAGB 18, Awe Inspiring Images 19; West Stow: 8; Wikimedia:
Meister des Book of Lindisfarne title page, Costumes of All
Nations (1882) Albert Kretschmer, painters and costumer
to the Royal Court Theatre, Berin, and Dr. Carl Rohrbach
7, Thomas Wright 10, Herbert Art Gallery and Museum,
Coventry 12t, portableantiquities 12b, Illustratedjc 20.

Every effort has been made to clear copyright.
Should there be any inadvertent omission,
please apply to the publisher for rectification.

The author, Izzi Howell, is a writer and editor specialising in children's educational publishing.

The consultant, Kate Ruttle, is a literacy expert and SENCO, and teaches in Suffolk.

FACT CAT FACT

There is a question for you to answer on each spread in this book. You can check your answers on page 24.

CONTENTS

WHO WERE THE ANGLO-SAXONS?

Around 400CE, a group of people called the Anglo-Saxons took control of England. The Anglo-Saxons **ruled** England until the Normans arrived in 1066.

This is what we think Anglo-Saxon soldiers looked like. They attacked the **Britons** and took over their land.

The Anglo-Saxons were made up of three **tribes**. The Jutes came from what is today called Denmark, and the Angles and the Saxons came from northern Germany.

Each tribe **settled** in a different area of England. Look at the map – can you work out which tribe settled in the north of England?

Northumbria

Mercia

East
Anglia

Wessex   Kent

Areas settled by
the Anglo-Saxons

← Angles

← Jutes

← Saxons

FACT CAT FACT

The word 'England' means
'land of the Angles' in
Old English.

KINGS AND RULERS

After the Anglo-Saxon **invasion**, England was divided into **kingdoms**. Each kingdom had its own warrior king. The biggest kingdoms were Northumbria and Mercia.

This statue shows Offa, an Anglo-Saxon king. Which kingdom did Offa rule?

Noblemen, called thanes, helped the king to rule each kingdom. Thanes owned land and lived in large houses. **Peasants** worked on the thane's land.

This drawing shows a thane on the left, a king in the centre, and a queen on the right.

FACT CAT FACT

Kings and thanes usually owned **slaves**. Slaves had a hard life. They had to do the most difficult work that nobody else wanted to do.

HOUSES AND VILLAGES

At first, most Anglo-Saxons lived in small villages. At the centre of the village was a large hall where the thane lived. Later, these villages turned into towns as more people came to live there.

This is a model of what we think an Anglo-Saxon village looked like.

Anglo-Saxon houses were made from wood, with straw roofs. At that time, glass was very hard to make, so houses didn't have any windows.

At the centre of each house was an open fire. This fire would be used for cooking and to keep the house warm. It was very smoky!

FACT CAT FACT

Many towns in England today have Anglo-Saxon names. 'Ham' means village in Anglo-Saxon. So Birmingham was once a small village! Can you find the names of other Anglo-Saxon towns?

FOOD AND COOKING

The Anglo-Saxons grew **crops** and kept animals such as cows and sheep for milk and meat. They also hunted **wild** animals such as deer and boar.

Farmers had to **plough** their fields before they could plant seeds. What type of animal is pulling the plough in this Anglo-Saxon drawing?

God spede þe plowȝ·ꝭ sende us koꝛne y nolk

Anglo-Saxons did most of their cooking on the open fires in their houses. However, they baked bread in an outdoor stone oven. Everyone who lived in the village shared one oven.

Anglo-Saxon women often cooked stews and soups. These dishes were left cooking all day while the women did other jobs, such as sewing or cleaning.

FACT CAT FACT

In Anglo-Saxon times, carrots were white or purple, not orange! Orange carrots weren't grown until the 17th century.

CRAFTS

Everything in an Anglo-Saxon home, from furniture to clothes, was made by village **craftsmen**. Some large towns even had goldsmiths and silversmiths, who made beautiful jewellery and armour for noblemen.

Blacksmiths made weapons and cooking pots from metal. This bowl has decorated handles, so it probably belonged to a rich thane.

These rings are made from gold and **gemstones**. Only rich people had enough money to pay for them.

Anglo-Saxon women made clothes for everyone in the family. First, they would make **yarn** from wool or plants. When they had enough yarn, they would **weave** it into fabric. This fabric would be made into clothes.

Anglo-Saxon women made yarn by twisting wool around a heavy piece of wood or bone. Which animal does most wool come from?

FACT CAT FACT

Anglo-Saxon peasants **dyed** their yarn red, yellow and blue using plants and berries. Bright purple dye was very hard to make, so only the king wore purple clothes.

RELIGION

The first Anglo-Saxons worshipped many gods and goddesses. Each looked after a different part of everyday life, such as war or families.

Frige

Woden

This painting shows the king of the Anglo-Saxon gods, Woden, and his wife Frige. Woden was the god of knowledge, and Frige was the goddess of love.

FACT CAT FACT

Many days of the week are named after Anglo-Saxon gods. Wednesday comes from 'Woden's day', and Thursday comes from 'Thunor's day'. Which Anglo-Saxon god is Friday named after?

Remains of an Anglo-Saxon cross

Around 600CE, a **powerful** Anglo-Saxon king decided to become a **Christian**. Over time, many Anglo-Saxons stopped worshipping their old gods and goddesses and became Christians too.

When the Anglo-Saxons became Christians, they started to build churches and **engraved** crosses. Some of these crosses are still standing today.

WEAPONS AND ARMOUR

Each Anglo-Saxon kingdom had its own small army, with around 100 soldiers. Kingdoms often fought each other because they wanted more land, or to show how strong they were.

This Anglo-Saxon solider is wearing metal armour and is carrying a shield to **protect** himself. What material were most Anglo-Saxon shields made from?

Most Anglo-Saxon soldiers fought with spears or axes, as swords were very expensive. They also carried small **daggers** in their belts.

This decorated helmet probably belonged to a powerful nobleman or king. Most ordinary Anglo-Saxon soldiers wore simple metal helmets.

FACT CAT **FACT**

Although the Anglo-Saxons travelled to their battlegrounds on horses, historians don't think that they rode their horses into battle.

KING ALFRED AND THE VIKINGS

In the 700s, Vikings from Denmark, Norway and Sweden started to attack Anglo-Saxon towns on the east coast of England. By the 800s, Vikings controlled many areas of England.

These are the ruins of Lindisfarne **monastery**, which was **destroyed** by the Vikings. What kind of people live in a monastery?

In 878, Alfred, the king of Wessex, decided to fight back against the Vikings. King Alfred's army won, but he decided to share England with the Vikings. He ruled south-west England, while the Vikings controlled the north-east.

This is a statue of King Alfred, also known as Alfred the Great. The Anglo-Saxons were happy when King Alfred made peace with the Vikings.

FACT CAT FACT

The peace with the Vikings didn't last long. One Anglo-Saxon king tried paying the Vikings to stay away, but it didn't work. There were many battles, and the Vikings even ruled all of England for a short time.

THE NORMANS ARRIVE

Harold Godwinson was the last Anglo-Saxon king.
Two of his enemies wanted to rule England – the
Viking king, Harald Hardrada, and William, a duke
from Normandy, in France.
Both Harald and William decided
to invade England in 1066.

Harald Hardrada's army attacked from the north. They were beaten by the Anglo-Saxons at the Battle of Stamford Bridge, shown here in this painting.

Harald Hardrada

A few weeks after Harald's army was beaten, William's army arrived on the south coast of England. There was a battle between the Anglo-Saxon and the Norman armies, near Hastings.

This drawing shows the moment when Harold Godwinson was killed by the Normans. After Harold's death, the Anglo-Saxon army **surrendered**. William became the first Norman king of England.

Harold Godwinson

FACT CAT FACT

William was crowned King of England on Christmas Day 1066! What name was given to William after he took control of England?

QUIZ

Try to answer the questions below. Look back through the book to help you. Check your answers on page 24.

1 Which Anglo-Saxon tribe came from Denmark?

a) Angles

b) Jutes

c) Saxons

2 Who helped the king to rule the kingdom?

a) peasants

b) slaves

c) thanes

3 Anglo-Saxon houses were made from brick. True or not true?

a) true

b) not true

4 The Anglo-Saxons were Christians when they first arrived in Britain. True or not true?

a) true

b) not true

5 Who started to attack the east coast of Britain in the 700s?

a) The Vikings

b) The Romans

c) The Saxons

6 William became the king of England in 1066. True or not true?

a) true

b) not true

GLOSSARY

blacksmith someone who is skilled at making things from metal, mainly iron

Briton a Celtic person; the Celts lived in Britain before and at the same time as the Romans

CE (common era) after the birth of Christ

Christian someone who believes in the Christian religion

craftsman someone who is skilled at making things by hand

crop a plant that farmers grow in large quantities

dagger a short knife used as a weapon

destroy damage something so badly that it doesn't exist anymore

dye to change the colour of something

engrave to cut words or pictures into stone or metal

gemstone a jewel or precious stone

invasion when an army enters a country, and takes control of it

kingdom an area ruled by a king or a queen

monastery a place where religious men, called monks, live together

nobleman a person who had a high position in society

Old English the language that was spoken by the Anglo-Saxons in Britain

peasant a poor person

plough a large tool used by farmers to dig and move soil, pulled by oxen or horses

powerful able to control people and events

protect to keep something safe

rule to control a country or an area

settle to start living in a new place and make it your home

slave someone who is owned by, and works for, another person

surrender to stop fighting and admit that you have lost

tribe a group of people who live together

weave to make cloth by passing threads over and under each other

wild living naturally and not looked after by humans

yarn thread used to make cloth

INDEX

ANSWERS

Pages 5–21

page 5: the Angles

page 6: Mercia

page 9: Some other towns include Norwich ('wich' is the Anglo-Saxon word for farm product)

page 10: a cow or an ox

page 13: sheep

page 14: Frige

page 16: wood

page 18: monks

page 21: William the Conqueror

Quiz answers

1   b) Jutes

2   c) thanes

3   b) not true. They were made from wood.

4   b) not true. They became Christians in the 600s.

5   a) the Vikings

6   a) true